Successfully
Building Your Brand with Instagram
By Jim Gerhardt

No portion of this book may be reproduced in any form without permission from the Author except as provided by U.S. Copyright law. Every effort has been made by the Author to ensure that the information contained in this book was correct as of release time. The Author and Publisher hereby disclaim and do not assume liability for any injury, loss, claim, damage or disruption caused by errors or omissions, regardless of whether any errors or omissions result from negligence, accident or any other causes. Readers are encouraged to verify any information contained in this book prior to taking any action on the information. Nothing in this book is legal advice.

For rights and permissions contact:
Jim Gerhardt
P.O. Box 583
Lexington, TN 38351
jgmerch.101@gmail.com

COPYRIGHT 2025 Jim Gerhardt ALL RIGHTS RESERVED

TABLE OF CONTENTS

Chapter 1: Understanding Instagram as a Branding Platform

Chapter 2: Defining Your Brand

Chapter 3: Creating a Winning Instagram Strategy

Chapter 4: Crafting Engaging Content

Chapter 5: Growing Your Audience

Chapter 6: Analyzing and Optimizing Your Performance

Chapter 7: Navigating Instagram Trends and Updates

Chapter 8: Success Stories and Case Studies

Chapter 9: Building Long-Term Brand Loyalty

Chapter 10: Scaling Beyond Instagram

Cliff Note Summary of "Successfully Building Your Brand with Instagram"

Top 10 Websites which also Promote Instagram Brand Growth

This Guide provides fundamental steps to grow your brand on Instagram while exploring its potential for businesses and personal branding. The chapters are structured to help readers strategize, create compelling content, engage audiences/customers and optimize performance. This comprehensive plan is an extremely valuable marketing tool..

Plan Your Work, then Work the Plan.

The proper attitude plus the proper consistent effort combined with a simple yet effective plan will create success. Your level of success will rely upon many factors, most of which You control. *Jim Gerhardt*

Chapter 1: Understanding Instagram as a Branding Platform

The Power of Instagram

Instagram's highly visual design makes it an ideal platform for branding. With over 1 billion monthly active users, businesses can reach global audiences through photo, video, and story-based content.

Unlike text-heavy platforms, Instagram lets brands connect emotionally with their audience through stunning visuals and creative storytelling.

Why Instagram?

Engagement: Instagram boasts higher engagement rates than other platforms. Posts and Stories facilitate direct interactions with audiences, creating real-time connections.

Discovery: Features like hashtags, Explore page, and geotags make it easy for new audiences to discover your content.

Tools: Business profiles gain access to Instagram Insights, Ads, and shopping tools that simplify building a seamless brand experience.

Understanding Instagram's Core Features

<u>Brands must familiarize themselves with Instagram's tools to maximize their presence</u>:

Posts: Great for curated, polished content to define your brand's aesthetic.

Stories: Temporary yet powerful for behind-the-scenes content, quick updates, or polls.

Reels: A hub for short-form, entertaining, and viral content.

IG Live: Direct interaction via live streaming, perfect for Q&A sessions or product launches.

Shopping Features: For retail brands, Instagram Shopping integrates product catalogs with your profile, allowing users to shop directly.

Instagram Demographics and Trends

Key Statistics:

Ages 18-34 dominate Instagram, making it crucial for brands targeting Millennials and Gen Z.

50% of users have made a purchase after seeing a product on Instagram.

Meta reports that 70% of shoppers use instagram to discover products, but not all convert immediately.

Industry metrics also show that many users discover products on Instagram but may purchase them later on other channels.

Current Trends:

Growth of video content: Reels outperform static posts in reach and engagement.

Authenticity matters: Audiences connect better with brands that appear genuine and relatable.

Chapter 2: Defining Your Brand

What is Your Brand Identity?

Brand identity is how your audience perceives your business. It's more than just a logo, it's a combination of your visuals, messaging, and the emotional connection you evoke.

Step 1: **Understand Your Audience**

Research your target audience's demographics, preferences, and pain points. Use tools like Instagram polls or analytics to gather insights.

Step 2: **Define Your Mission and Values**

Clearly articulate what your brand stands for. Ask yourself: What do we want to achieve, and why?
Example: A sustainable fashion brand's mission might focus on ethical production and eco-consciousness.

Step 3: **Build a Brand Voice**

Your tone and style of communication must align with your audience's expectations.
Casual and humorous? Ideal for lifestyle brands targeting younger audiences.
Formal and informative? Suitable for financial or professional services.

Building Your Visual Identity

Consistent Color Palette: Use 3-5 colors that represent your brand and apply them across posts, Stories, and highlights.

Typography: Fonts communicate personality. A playful sans-serif may fit a children's brand, while a sleek serif font suits luxury products.

Photography Style: Decide on specific filters or editing techniques to maintain cohesion.

Logo Placement: Use your logo sparingly in posts but consistently in profile pictures and IG Stories Highlights covers.

Chapter 3: Creating a Winning Instagram Strategy

Setting Goals for Your Instagram Presence

To succeed, **define clear objectives**. Examples include:

1. Growing brand awareness by reaching 50,000 followers in 6 months.

2. Boosting website traffic by 30% through Instagram ads and bio links.

3. Generating leads via interactive Story stickers like quizzes or polls.

Set daily, monthly, yearly, etc. goals. Maintain a consistent work schedule.

Developing a Content Calendar

Consistency is key to success.

A content calendar helps organize themes, posting frequency, and content types.

Monthly Themes: Align content with seasonal trends, product launches, or campaigns.

Post Variety: Mix educational content, behind-the-scenes glimpses, and user-generated posts.

Aligning with Instagram's Algorithm

Instagram prioritizes posts based on:

Relevance: Are your posts aligned with the user's interests?

Engagement: High likes, shares, and comments boost visibility.

Consistency: Regular posting signals activity to Instagram's algorithm.

Always use quality content. Regular engagement is great but if the content is not great, you might lose more followers than you gain.

A Quality Brand requires quality content.

Chapter 4: Crafting Engaging Content

Types of Content that Work

From photo posts to Stories, Reels, and live sessions, this chapter delves into the types of content that help brands thrive on Instagram.

Writing Captions that Convert

Tips for writing captions that boost engagement, tell a compelling story, or drive your audience to take action.

Using Hashtags Effectively

Learn how to research and use hashtags strategically to reach the right audience without overloading your posts.

Instagram's visual nature and dynamic features make it a goldmine for content creators and brands. But success on this platform requires more than just beautiful images—it's about **delivering consistent, engaging, and memorable content** that aligns with your brand's mission and captivates your audience.

This chapter will explore the types of content that excel on Instagram and offer actionable tips for writing captions that resonate and convert.

Types of Content that Work

Instagram offers a versatile range of content formats, each with unique benefits. Mastering these formats can help you maximize reach and engagement while staying relevant in a fast-paced digital world.

1. Photo Posts: The Classic Foundation

High-quality photo posts remain a staple of Instagram. Whether showcasing a product, a behind-the-scenes moment, or an aspirational lifestyle shot, photos are often the first impression your brand makes.

Tips for success:

Use natural lighting and a consistent color palette to create a cohesive feed.

Highlight textures, details, or emotions to evoke curiosity or connection.

Experiment with composition techniques like the rule of thirds or symmetrical framing.

2. Instagram Stories: Authentic and Ephemeral

Stories are an excellent way to connect with your audience through real-time, unpolished content. These 24-hour snippets allow you to share updates, run polls, or offer exclusive deals.

Ideas for Stories:

Host "a day in the life" or "behind the scenes" features.

Use interactive elements like question boxes, quizzes, or polls.

Share user-generated content (UGC) to spotlight loyal customers.

3. Reels: Short-Form Storytelling

As Instagram leans into video, Reels offer a creative way to showcase products, entertain followers, or educate your audience. The algorithm favors Reels, making them a powerful tool for reaching new users.

Pro tips:

Keep videos between 7–15 seconds for optimal engagement.

Pair trending audio with original visuals for a broader reach.

Include captions or subtitles to make your content accessible.

4. Live Sessions: Real-Time Interaction

Live videos foster a sense of community by allowing direct interaction with your audience. Use Lives to host Q & A sessions, launch new products or collaborate with influencers.

Best practices:

Promote your **"Live"** in advance to ensure viewers tune in.

Engage viewers by answering their questions in real-time.

Repurpose the recording as an IGTV video for long-term value.

Writing **Captions That Convert**

While stunning visuals grab attention, it's your captions that keep your audience engaged and drive action. A well-crafted caption can tell a story, evoke emotions, and prompt your followers to take specific steps.

1. **Start Strong with a Hook**

Instagram captions are truncated after a few lines, so the first sentence is crucial. Open with an intriguing question, bold statement, or compelling fact to encourage followers to read more.

Example: "Struggling to find the perfect holiday gift? We've got you covered with these 5 must-haves!"

2. **Know Your Goal**

<u>Define the purpose of your caption before writing</u>. Are you trying to educate, entertain, or sell? Tailor your language accordingly.

Educational captions: Use a "how-to" format or share tips.

Entertaining captions: Incorporate humor, memes, or trending topics.

Sales-focused captions: Highlight benefits and include a **clear call-to-action** (CTA).

3. **Incorporate Storytelling**

Storytelling helps humanize your brand and make it relatable. Share a personal anecdote, a customer testimonial, or the journey behind your product.

Example: "When we started designing this backpack, we thought about all the little inconveniences you face during travel.

Fast forward two years, and here's the result—a bag that adapts to your needs."

4. Use Emojis Strategically

Emojis add personality and break up text, making captions easier to read. Use them sparingly to emphasize key points or match your brand voice.

Example: "🌟 Big news! We're launching our new collection this Friday.

Stay tuned for exclusive offers! "

5. *Include a Call-to-Action (CTA)*

Every caption should encourage the audience to take a next step, whether it's liking the post, sharing it, or visiting your website.

Effective CTAs:

A. "Double-tap if you agree!"

B. "Tag a friend who needs to see this!"

C. "Click the link in our bio to shop now!"

6. Write for Your Audience

Use language and tone that align with your target audience. A formal caption may suit a luxury brand, while a casual, playful tone works better for lifestyle brands.

Putting It All Together

Crafting engaging Instagram content requires balance: the right visuals, an authentic voice, and actionable captions. Imagine you're a skincare brand:

Photo: A close-up of a glowing face with your product prominently displayed. Always use high quality images focused on your message.

Caption: "Struggling with winter dryness? Our hydrating serum is here to rescue your skin. Packed with hyaluronic acid, it locks in moisture for up to 24 hours. Tap the link in bio to shop now!"

By consistently experimenting with content types and honing your caption-writing skills, you'll not only build a loyal audience but also turn followers into advocates for your brand.

Chapter 5: Growing Your Audience

Organic Growth Strategies

Explore the role of engagement tactics like replying to comments, participating in challenges, and cross-promoting your content.

Collaborations and Influencer Marketing

Understand how to collaborate with influencers or complementary brands to expand your reach and build credibility.

Paid Promotions

Learn how Instagram ads work, how to create effective campaigns, and measure their success.

When you spend money on ads ensure that your ads are increasing profits or the metrics/traffic that results in sales.

Building an audience on Instagram is about more than just accumulating followers—it's about **cultivating a community of engaged users who trust your brand** and resonate with your message. In this chapter, we'll cover proven strategies to grow your audience, including organic engagement tactics, collaborations, and paid promotions.

https://payhip.com/JGMerch1

Organic Growth Strategies

Organic growth is the foundation of building an authentic and loyal audience. Unlike paid promotions, it requires time and effort but yields deeper connections with your followers.

1. Engage Consistently

Engagement is a two-way street on Instagram. Actively responding to your audience fosters trust and shows that you value their input.

Reply to Comments: Take time to reply to comments on your posts. Even a simple "Thank you!" or a personalized response can make followers feel appreciated.

DM Conversations: If a follower sends you a direct message or tags you in a story, respond promptly and thoughtfully.

Engage on Their Content: Visit the profiles of your followers or potential followers and interact with their posts by liking, commenting, or sharing meaningful feedback.

2. Participate in Instagram Challenges

Instagram challenges are a creative way to increase visibility and attract like-minded users. Whether it's a fitness challenge, a themed photo series, or a hashtag-driven trend, participating shows that your brand is active and relatable.

Example:
If you're a fitness brand, join or create challenges like #30DayWellnessChallenge to connect with health-conscious users.

3. Use Hashtags Strategically

Hashtags categorize your content and make it discoverable to new audiences.

Combine broad hashtags (e.g., #FitnessGoals) with niche hashtags (e.g., #MorningYogaRoutine) to target both general and specific audiences.

Research trending hashtags in your industry, but avoid overloading your post with irrelevant tags.

4. Cross-Promote Your Content

Leveraging other platforms and formats can drive traffic to your Instagram account.

Share on Other Social Media: Post teasers of your Instagram content on Facebook, LinkedIn, or Twitter to encourage your audience to follow you.

Embed Instagram Posts on Your Website: If you have a blog or website, embed your Instagram feed to showcase your latest updates.

When you post on Instagram you have the option to share that content to Facebook.

This is an easy way to extend your marketing footprint. Facebook is also a great tool for marketing and sales.

Collaborate With Partners: Tagging and being tagged by collaborators can introduce your brand to their audience.

Collaborations and Influencer Marketing

Collaborations can significantly amplify your reach by exposing your brand to new and relevant audiences. The key is to partner with individuals or brands that align with your values and resonate with your target market.

1. **Identify the Right Influencers**

An effective collaboration starts with finding influencers who share your brand's values and have genuine connections with their followers.

Micro-Influencers (10,000–50,000 followers): These influencers often have niche audiences with high engagement rates, making them ideal for smaller brands.

Macro-Influencers (100,000+ followers): While their reach is broader, engagement rates may vary. Use these partnerships for campaigns aiming at mass exposure.

2. Collaborate With Complementary Brands

Partnering with non-competing brands that share a similar audience can be a win-win.

Example: A skincare brand could collaborate with a wellness brand to co-host a giveaway or cross-promote products in Stories.

Joint Campaign Ideas: Host a live Q&A together, create bundled product offers, or share each other's content.

3. Execute Successful Influencer Campaigns

To ensure a partnership delivers results, define clear objectives and provide creative freedom.

Set Goals: Are you aiming for brand awareness, lead generation, or direct sales?

Track Metrics: Use tools like Instagram Insights or third-party analytics to monitor impressions, engagement, and conversions.

Provide Guidance: Share your brand voice, key messages, and any non-negotiable guidelines while allowing influencers to speak authentically to their audience.

Paid Promotions

When organic strategies reach their limits, paid promotions can help you target a wider audience quickly and effectively. Instagram Ads offer various formats to suit your campaign goals.

1. How Instagram Ads Work

Instagram ads are powered by Meta's advertising platform, allowing you to target users based on demographics, interests, behavior, and more. Ads can appear in users' feeds, Stories, Explore pages, or Reels.

Ad Formats:

Photo Ads: Showcase products or services with striking visuals.

Video Ads: Ideal for storytelling or demonstrating a product in action.

Carousel Ads: Allow users to swipe through multiple images or videos in one ad.

Story Ads: Full-screen, immersive ads that appear between user Stories.

2. **Creating Effective Campaigns**

Successful ad campaigns rely on a combination of eye-catching visuals, compelling messaging, and precise targeting.

Define Your Audience: Use Instagram's targeting tools to select age, location, interests, and behaviors. Narrow your focus to avoid wasting your budget.

Craft a Clear CTA: Whether it's "Shop Now," "Learn More," or "Sign Up," make your CTA (Call to Action) easy to understand and action-oriented.

A/B Testing: Experiment with different visuals, headlines, and CTAs to determine what resonates most with your audience.

3. **Measuring Ad Success**

Analyzing your ad performance is critical for optimizing future campaigns.

Use metrics like:

Impressions: How many times your ad was displayed.

Engagement Rate: The percentage of users who liked, commented, or shared the ad.

Click-Through Rate (CTR): The ratio of users who clicked your ad's link.

Return on Ad Spend (ROAS): Measure the revenue generated relative to your ad spend.

Putting It All Together

Growing your audience on Instagram isn't about quick fixes; it's about leveraging a blend of organic strategies, collaborative partnerships, and targeted paid campaigns. Here's an example of a comprehensive growth strategy for a small wellness brand:

1. Organic Strategy: Post daily tips and use hashtags like #SelfCareDaily. Engage with followers through polls and Q&As in Stories.

2. Collaborations: Partner with a yoga instructor to host an Instagram Live on stress relief techniques.

3. Paid Promotions: Run a Story ad campaign promoting a limited-time offer on your best-selling product.

- By consistently applying these strategies and refining them based on your analytics, you will have a much greater chance of success in building your Brand and Profits.

Chapter 6: Analyzing and Optimizing Your Performance

Instagram Analytics 101

Dive into Instagram Insights and other tools to track your content performance, audience behavior, and overall account growth.

Adjusting Your Strategy Based on Data
Learn how to pivot your approach based on analytics, audience feedback, and new trends on Instagram.

Success on Instagram requires more than just posting great content. To truly build your brand, you need to understand what's working, what's not, and how to refine your approach over time.

This chapter explores the tools available to track your performance and how to use data-driven insights to optimize your strategy.

Instagram Analytics METRICS 101

Instagram provides powerful tools to help you analyze your content performance, audience behavior, and account growth. Understanding these metrics will allow you to make informed decisions and continuously improve your results.

1. Accessing Instagram Insights

Instagram Insights is a built-in analytics tool available to business and creator accounts.

To access it:

Go to your profile and tap the Insights button.

Navigate through categories like Content, Activity, and Audience.

2. **Key Metrics to Monitor**

Here's a breakdown of essential metrics and what they tell you:

Content Metrics:

Reach: The total number of unique users who saw your post.

Impressions: The total number of times your content was displayed, including repeat views.

Engagement Rate: A percentage calculated by dividing total interactions (likes, comments, shares, saves) by total reach.

A high engagement rate indicates your content resonates with your audience.

Audience Metrics:

Follower Demographics: Learn about your audience's age, gender, and location to tailor content accordingly.

Active Times: See when your followers are most active to post at optimal times.

Activity Metrics:

Profile Visits: Track how many users visited your profile after seeing your content.

Website Clicks: Measure how many users clicked the link in your bio, indicating successful call-to-actions (CTAs).

3. Third-Party Analytics Tools

While Instagram Insights is robust, third-party tools can offer additional features:

Hootsuite: Provides detailed scheduling and performance tracking across multiple platforms.

Sprout Social: Offers competitor analysis and audience listening tools.
Later: Focuses on visual planning with integrated analytics.

Adjusting Your Strategy Based on Data

Analytics provide the foundation for smart decision-making. Use the data to identify trends, address weaknesses, and capitalize on opportunities.

1. Identifying What Works

Study your top-performing posts to uncover patterns:

What type of content receives the most engagement (photos, videos, Reels, Stories)?

Do certain topics, hashtags, or captions consistently outperform others?

Is there a specific time of day when your audience is most active?

Example: If Reels are driving the most engagement, allocate more resources to producing short-form videos.

2. Addressing Weak Spots

Underperforming content can offer valuable lessons. Ask yourself:

Was the caption engaging enough?

Did the visuals align with your brand's aesthetic?

Could the timing or hashtags have been improved?

Action Step: Experiment with different formats or styles to identify what resonates better with your audience.

3. Listening to Audience Feedback

Direct engagement with your audience is another critical data point. Pay attention to comments, DMs, and poll responses to understand their preferences.

Polls and Q&A Features: Use Instagram Stories to ask your followers what they want to see more of.

Comment Sentiment Analysis: Are the comments positive, neutral, or critical? Adjust your tone or content focus accordingly.

4. Staying Ahead of Trends

Instagram is constantly evolving, introducing new features like Reels, Guides, and AI-assisted tools. Keep your strategy flexible to adapt to changes.

Stay Updated: Follow Instagram's official blog or social media channels for updates.

Experiment Early: Test new features as they roll out to gain an edge over competitors.

Optimizing for Long-Term Growth

Optimization isn't a one-time effort—it's an ongoing process that requires regular evaluation and adjustment.

1. Set SMART Goals

Define Specific, Measurable, Achievable, Relevant, and Time-bound goals to focus your efforts.

Example Goals:

Increase engagement rate by 10% over three months.

Gain 1,000 new followers by the end of the quarter.

Drive 15% more website traffic through Instagram within six weeks.

2. Test and Refine

Use A/B testing to experiment with different content variables:

Test different CTAs: "Shop Now" vs. "Learn More."

Experiment with posting times to find your audience's peak engagement periods.

Compare the performance of professional photos against user-generated content.

3. Measure Return on Investment (ROI)

If you're investing in paid promotions, ensure the returns justify the costs.
Track the direct impact of ads on sales, sign-ups, or website traffic.
Use tools like Google Analytics to correlate Instagram traffic with conversions.

4. Regular Performance Audits

Schedule monthly or quarterly reviews to analyze progress against your goals. Create reports that highlight:
Overall account growth (follower count, reach).
Content engagement trends.
Success of campaigns or collaborations.

Case Study: Turning Data Into Success

Brand: A small eco-friendly clothing company noticed their posts featuring sustainability tips performed better than product shots.

Action: They shifted their content strategy to include more educational posts about eco-friendly living.

Result: Engagement rates increased by 25%, and website clicks doubled within two months.

Final Thoughts

Analyzing and optimizing your performance on Instagram is the key to sustained growth and relevance. By leveraging analytics to refine your content strategy, engaging with audience feedback, and staying adaptable to trends, you can ensure that your efforts consistently yield results.

Chapter 7: Navigating Instagram Trends and Updates

Keeping Up with Platform Changes

Stay ahead of the curve by adapting to Instagram's algorithm changes, new features, and shifts in user behavior.

Integrating Emerging Trends

This section provides actionable advice on how to incorporate trends like augmented reality filters, interactive polls, or AI into your branding strategy.

Instagram is a dynamic platform that evolves rapidly with new features, algorithm changes, and emerging user behaviors. Staying ahead of these trends is crucial for maintaining visibility, engagement, and relevance.

In this chapter, you'll learn how to adapt to platform updates and leverage trends to enhance your brand's presence.

Keeping Up with Platform Changes

Instagram frequently rolls out updates that can significantly impact how users interact with content. From algorithm adjustments to feature launches, understanding these changes is essential to staying competitive.

1. Understanding the Instagram Algorithm

The Instagram algorithm determines the content users see in their feeds, Explore pages, and Reels. Staying visible means working with, not against, the algorithm.

Key Algorithm Factors:

Engagement: Posts with higher likes, comments, and shares are prioritized.

Relevance: The algorithm favors content that matches user interests based on their activity.

Timeliness: Fresh content is more likely to appear in users' feeds.

Tips to Thrive:

Encourage engagement through CTAs in captions (e.g., "What do you think? Comment below!").

Post consistently to stay top-of-mind. Familiarity often enhances trust.

Use hashtags to increase discoverability.

2. Staying Informed About Updates

Instagram often announces changes through their blog or social media channels. Make it a habit to stay informed:

Follow Instagram Creators Account (@creators): This account highlights new features and best practices.

Subscribe to Industry Newsletters: Platforms like Social Media Examiner or Later provide insights on Instagram updates.

Experiment Early: Early adopters of new features often gain an edge, as Instagram tends to prioritize fresh functionalities in the algorithm.

3. Adapting to New Features

Every new feature presents an opportunity to connect with your audience in innovative ways. Recent examples include:

Reels: Short, engaging videos that often reach a broader audience than static posts.

Collaborative Posts: Allowing two accounts to share the same post, increasing exposure for both.

Enhanced Messaging Tools: Using DM automation or interactive quick replies to engage followers more efficiently.

Example: A fitness brand could use Reels to showcase quick workout tips, leveraging the feature's preference for video content to attract a wider audience.

Integrating Emerging Trends

Capitalizing on trends is a great way to keep your content fresh and aligned with audience interests. Successful brands don't just follow trends, they adapt them to fit their unique voice and goals.

1. Leverage Augmented Reality (AR) Features

Instagram's AR filters are a fun and interactive way to engage your audience.

Custom Filters: Create branded filters that align with your niche, such as a filter showing your logo or a product demo.

Interactive Experiences: Encourage followers to use your filters and tag your brand in their posts.

Example: A beauty brand could design a filter that allows users to "try on" different makeup looks virtually, driving interest in their products.

2. Engage With Interactive Features

Interactive tools like polls, quizzes, and question stickers allow you to connect with followers and gather valuable feedback.

Polls: Ask your audience to vote on new product ideas, creating a sense of ownership and engagement.

Quizzes: Test followers' knowledge about your niche while reinforcing your brand's expertise.

Countdown Stickers: Build excitement for events like product launches or sales.

Example: A food brand could use polls in Stories to ask followers about their favorite flavors, driving excitement for a new product release.

3. Tap Into AI and Automation

Artificial intelligence is transforming how brands interact on Instagram, from personalized DMs to content creation.

Chatbots for DMs: Automate responses to common queries while maintaining a personal touch.

AI-Generated Captions or Hashtags: Use AI tools to create captions or suggest trending hashtags, saving time and boosting visibility.

4. Ride the Wave of Cultural Trends

Staying in tune with broader cultural movements helps your brand remain relevant and relatable.

Seasonal Content: Post themed content for holidays, seasons, or major events.

Social Movements: Align with causes that resonate with your brand values, but ensure your support is genuine and backed by action.

Memes and Pop Culture References: Incorporate humor or timely references to connect with younger audiences.

Caution: Ensure that your participation in trends aligns with your brand identity and audience expectations.

Building a Trend-Ready Strategy

1. Stay Flexible and Experimental

The best strategies are adaptable. Test new trends, analyze the results, and decide what works for your audience.

Track metrics like reach, engagement, and follower growth to determine the impact of new trends on your content.

Be willing to pivot if a trend isn't yielding results.

2. Focus on Authenticity

While trends can boost visibility, authenticity is key to maintaining credibility. Ensure that every trend you participate in aligns with your brand's core values.

3. Plan Ahead for Trends

Many trends are predictable, such as holiday campaigns or annual events like Instagram's Year in Review. Plan content around these moments to stay ahead of the curve.

4. Collaborate With Trendsetters

Work with influencers or creators who are early adopters of trends. Their expertise and following can help your brand stay ahead of the game.

Case Study: A Small Brand's Trend Success

Brand: A boutique coffee shop noticed the rise of AR filters and decided to create one that allowed users to "guess their coffee personality."
Action: The filter was shared across Stories, and users tagged the brand when using it.

Result: The filter gained traction, leading to a 30% increase in profile visits and a 15% boost in follower count within two weeks.

In Summary

Navigating Instagram trends and updates can feel overwhelming, but it's also an exciting opportunity to showcase your brand's creativity and adaptability.

By staying informed, experimenting with new features, and integrating trends in a way that aligns with your brand's values, you'll ensure your Instagram strategy remains relevant and impactful.

Chapter 8: Success Stories and Case Studies

Brands That Built Their Empire on Instagram

Glossier:

Known for their clean and minimalist aesthetic.

Embraced user-generated content by sharing followers' makeup selfies, which built a loyal community.

Gymshark:

Leveraged influencers and fitness enthusiasts to promote activewear.

Shared workout tips and motivational posts to engage followers.

National Geographic:

Tells stories through stunning photography.

Balances environmental advocacy with visually captivating content.

Key Takeaways:

Authenticity and storytelling drive engagement.

Leverage collaborations to expand reach.

Use a mix of formats: Reels, IGTV, and Stories.

Chapter 9: Building Long-Term Brand Loyalty

Nurturing Your Audience

Your Instagram followers are more than numbers. They are potential brand ambassadors.

Create a bond by:

Engaging directly with comments and messages.

Featuring user-generated content to validate your audience's contributions.

Hosting interactive Q&A sessions to build personal connections.

Encouraging User-Generated Content (UGC)

Involve your audience in your brand's story:

Launch hashtag campaigns (e.g., #ShareYourStyle).

Share customer reviews or unboxing videos.

Organize contests and giveaways for tagged photos.

Building Trust Through Transparency

Modern consumers **value authenticity**. Share behind-the-scenes content showing product creation, team members, or business processes.

Use Stories and Reels to humanize your brand.

Chapter 10: Scaling Beyond Instagram

Expanding to Other Platforms

Once your Instagram branding strategy is strong, use it to build a multi-platform presence:

TikTok: A great compliment for short, viral video content.

Pinterest: Ideal for showcasing product catalogs and DIY inspiration.

LinkedIn: Share professional milestones and industry insights for B2B branding.

Creating a Seamless Brand Ecosystem

Ensure your branding remains consistent across all platforms, from visuals to tone.

Drive traffic between platforms (e.g., promote YouTube videos via Instagram Stories).

Establish a website as your central hub, using Instagram for lead generation.

Launching Products and Services

Use Instagram as a springboard for broader ventures:

Announce launches with teaser Reels or countdown stickers.

Host IG Lives for product demonstrations or Q&A sessions.

Utilize Instagram Shops to drive sales.

Conclusion

This structure provides a complete roadmap for readers looking to harness the power of Instagram to build a strong, successful brand, whether they're entrepreneurs, content creators or small business owners.

The primary building block of Building Your Brand with Instagram and your marketing success is that you must understand what's happening in your market, who your ideal prospect is, what they're most interested in and the type of content which engages them with your Brand, product or service.

Focus each post or reel on who your ideal prospects are for that specific product or service.

Review what your competition is doing on Instagram.

Focus your content on your specific customers.

Advertise or market your company and your products based upon specific content which will get the most engagement from your target customers.

Once you have content which actually engages your Target customer base then you should be very consistent. <u>Set a specific schedule to which you post quality content</u>.

When your Target customer views your content on a regular basis that increases their trust and the rapport that you are creating by consistently engaging with them.

Plan your work, then work the plan.

Your success is largely determined by your proper attitude and proper consistent effort coupled with a quality product and an effective marketing-sales plan. The level of success that you achieve will rely upon many factors, most of which You control.

Good selling and All the Best,

Jim Gerhardt

Practical Worksheets and Templates follow the Citations.

Citations

1. SocialBee - How to Build Your Brand 【6】

2. OnlySocial - Building a Brand on Instagram 【7】

3. HubSpot - Instagram Branding Strategies 【8】

4. Sked Social - Optimizing Instagram Presence 【9】

5. Hootsuite - Instagram Best Practices 【10】

Practical Worksheets and Templates for Readers

Chapter 1: Understanding Instagram as a Branding Platform

A. Instagram Platform Audit Worksheet

Assess your existing Instagram presence:

Current follower count

Engagement rate (likes/comments per post)

Profile completeness (bio, profile picture, highlights)

Identify areas for improvement

B. Competitor Analysis Template

Fields to compare:

Competitor handle

Visual style (colors, themes, post types)

Engagement levels

Popular content formats

Lessons to adapt

Chapter 2: Defining Your Brand

A. Brand Identity Blueprint

Brand Mission Statement:

What is your purpose and core values?

Audience Personal Template:

Name:

Age:

Location:

Interests:

Instagram habits:

Visual Style Planner:

Color Palette: Select 3-5 core colors.

Fonts: List primary and secondary typefaces.

Imagery Style: Describe photography or graphic preferences.

B. Brand Voice Worksheet

How would your brand sound in:

Captions? (e.g., humorous, formal, inspiring)

Responses to comments?

Instagram Stories?

Chapter 3: Creating a Winning Instagram Strategy

A. Content Goal Setting Template

Goal Categories:

Increase followers: [specific target]

Boost engagement rate: [specific percentage]

Drive traffic: [specific link clicks or website visits]

Timeframes and Milestones: Define timelines to achieve these goals.

B. Monthly Content Calendar Template

Columns:

Date

Post Type (Reel, Story, Carousel)

Caption Idea

Hashtags

Call-to-Action

Scheduled Time

C. Post Performance Tracker

Fields:

Date of Post

Likes
Comments
Shares
Saves
Reach

Chapter 8: Success Stories and Case Studies

A. Success Story Inspiration Worksheet

Analyze success stories:

What industry is this brand in?

What made their Instagram strategy unique?

Which elements of their approach can you adapt for your brand?

B. Collaboration Planning Template

Identify potential partners:

Influencers: [List their handles and follower counts]

Brands with similar values: [List 5 examples]

Outline partnership benefits for both sides.

Chapter 9: Building Long-Term Brand Loyalty

A. Audience Engagement Plan

Daily Tasks:

Respond to comments and DMs.

Like and comment on followers' posts.

Weekly Tasks:

Post an interactive Story (poll, quiz, or Q&A).

Share a user-generated post.

Monthly Tasks:

Host a giveaway or challenge.

B. UGC Campaign Template

Campaign Name:

Campaign Hashtag:

User Guidelines: What type of content to create and share.

Incentives: Rewards for participation (e.g., discounts, shoutouts).

C. Feedback Collection Form

Create an Instagram poll or form to ask:

What content do you enjoy most from our brand?

What can we do better?

Chapter 10: Scaling Beyond Instagram

A. Multi-Platform Branding Worksheet

Ensure consistent branding:

Instagram Handle: [@YourBrand]

TikTok Handle: [@YourBrand]

Pinterest Profile: [Your Brand Name]

Identify content unique to each platform.

B. Cross-Promotion Template

Identify key links to share:

YouTube videos

Blog posts

Email sign-up forms

Draft captions for promoting these links on Instagram.

C. Product Launch Checklist

Pre-Launch:

Teaser Reel or countdown Story posted?

Announcement date set?

Launch Day:

IG Live or launch Reel prepared?

Shopping link added to bio or Shop feature?

Post-Launch:

Collect user reviews via Stories or posts.

Cliff Notes Summary of This Book:

Successfully Building Your Brand with Instagram

Jim Gerhardt's *Successfully Building Your Brand with Instagram* is a step-by-step guide for entrepreneurs, content creators, and small business owners aiming to harness Instagram's potential for brand growth. The book outlines a structured approach to building, engaging, and monetizing a strong brand presence on one of the world's most influential social media platforms.

1. Instagram as a Branding Powerhouse

Instagram's visual nature and massive user base (primarily ages 18–34) make it ideal for emotional storytelling and community-building. With features like Stories, Reels, IG Live, and Shopping, brands can engage users in diverse and dynamic ways.

2. Defining Your Brand Identity

This Manual stresses the importance of clarity in branding—establishing a unique voice, mission, and visual identity. Understanding your target audience's demographics and pain points is essential. Consistent use of colors, fonts, and tone helps create a recognizable and trusted presence.

3. Strategic Content Planning

Success comes from setting clear, measurable goals (e.g., increasing engagement or traffic), using a content calendar, and aligning posts with Instagram's algorithm which favors consistency, engagement, and relevance.

4. Crafting Engaging Content

Effective Instagram content includes high-quality photos, interactive Stories, short-form Reels, and real-time IG Live sessions. Captions should open with a hook, include a clear call-to-action, use emojis sparingly, and always match the brand's tone.

5. Growing Your Audience

Gerhardt details both organic and paid strategies. Organically, engaging with followers, using challenges and strategic hashtags, and cross-promoting on other platforms help build community. Collaborations with influencers or like-minded brands amplify reach. Paid promotions should be precisely targeted, visually appealing, and tracked via analytics for ROI.

6. Performance Analytics & Optimization

Data drives strategy. Using Instagram Insights and third-party tools, brands can analyze reach, engagement, and audience behavior to refine content and posting schedules. SMART goals and A/B testing help optimize long-term performance.

7. Adapting to Trends

Staying relevant means embracing new features (like AR filters, Reels, and interactive tools) and aligning content with cultural trends, while maintaining authenticity.

8. Success Stories & Loyalty Building

Brands like Glossier, Gymshark, and National Geographic illustrate how storytelling, user-generated content (UGC), and influencer partnerships build massive followings. Loyalty comes from transparency, active engagement, and consistent value.

9. Scaling Beyond Instagram

Once a brand is established, Gerhardt recommends expanding to platforms like TikTok, Pinterest, or LinkedIn while keeping branding consistent. Instagram remains a central hub for lead generation and product launches.

Conclusion:

This guide emphasizes a practical mantra: *Plan your work, then work the plan.*

With consistent effort, a clear brand message, and data-informed strategies, success on Instagram is attainable and scalable.

Top Websites for Learning to Build Your Instagram Brand

1. **Later.com**

   - **Focus:** Instagram strategy, content planning, and visual scheduling.
   - **Highlights:** Blog, free Instagram tools, success stories, and tutorials on Reels, captions, and trends
   - .

2. **Hootsuite Blog**

   - **Focus:** Social media management and analytics.
   - **Highlights:** Instagram algorithm updates, growth hacks, and marketing playbooks.

3. **Social Media Examiner**

   - **Focus:** Social media marketing insights for professionals.
   - **Highlights:** In-depth guides on Instagram marketing, influencer strategies, and content creation tips.

4. **HubSpot Marketing Blog**

   - **Focus:** Inbound marketing and branding across platforms.
   - **Highlights:** Strategic branding guides, Instagram growth tips, and analytics tutorials.

5. **Sprout Social Insights**

    - **Focus:** Social listening, engagement metrics, and strategy.
    - **Highlights:** Instagram best practices, scheduling insights, and brand voice development.
    -

6. **Canva Design School**

    - **Focus:** Visual branding and graphic design for social media.
    - **Highlights:** Instagram templates, storytelling design tips, and branding consistency advice.

7. **Tailwind Blog**

    - **Focus:** Visual content marketing and social growth tools.
    - **Highlights:** Hashtag strategies, growth tracking, and Instagram content ideas.

8. **Neil Patel Blog**

    - **Focus:** Digital marketing, SEO, and content growth.
    - **Highlights:** Instagram growth tactics, monetization, and organic engagement strategies.

9. **Instagram for Business (Meta)**

    - **Focus:** Official business resources from Instagram/Meta.
    - **Highlights:** Case studies, tutorials, tools (like Insights and Ads), and new feature rollouts.

10. **SocialBee Blog**

    - **Focus:** Social media content planning and audience growth.

- **Highlights:** Instagram workflows, branding checklists, and automation strategies.

Each of these sites regularly publishes updated, data-backed content and many offer **free resources** such as templates, courses, and webinars to help elevate your brand.

Copyright 2025   Jim Gerhardt   ALL RIGHTS RESERVED

No portion of this book may be reproduced in any form without permission from the Author / Publisher, except as provided by U.S. copyright law.

Every effort has been made by the Author and publishing house to ensure that the information contained in this book was correct as of release time. The Author and publishing house hereby disclaim and do not assume liability for any injury, loss, damage, or disruption caused by errors or omissions, regardless of whether any errors or omissions result from negligence, accident or any other causes. Readers are encouraged to verify any information contained in this book prior to taking any action on the information. Nothing in this book is legal advice.

For rights and permissions, please contact:
Jim Gerhardt
P.O .Box 583
Lexington, TN 38351
JGMerch.101@gmail.com

Jim Gerhardt's Books, Podcasts and Training Materials
https://payhip.com/JGMerch1

Amazon Books (Kindle eBooks and Paperback Books)
https://www.amazon.com/**author**/jim_gerhardt

JGMerch1 online eStore
https://jgmerch1.etsy.com

About the Author, **Jim Gerhardt**

With over 30 years of expertise in marketing, sales, sales management and writing, Jim Gerhardt has built a career around helping individuals and businesses achieve success. As the author of several acclaimed books, ranging from technical and training guides to drama and mystery, He has a unique ability to simplify complex topics and captivate audiences.

Passionate about making a difference, he actively supports two vital causes: Animal rights and Veterans' care. In his latest book, Successfully Building Your Brand with Instagram, he leverages decades of experience to provide actionable insights for harnessing the power of social media to grow your brand, increase sales and connect with your audience.

Favorite Quote:

"When you arise in the morning, think of what a privilege it is to be alive, to think, to enjoy, to love ..."

~ Marcus Aurelius

Copyright 2025   Jim Gerhardt   ALL RIGHTS RESERVED

www.ingramcontent.com/pod-product-compliance
Lightning Source LLC
Chambersburg PA
CBHW071107240526
45469CB00006BD/2365